EXPERIENCING *the* REALITY
of TRUE MINISTRY

33DAYS
of STEWARDSHIP
DISCOVERY GUIDE

FINDING *and* FULFILLING
YOUR ROLE AS A STEWARD
of GOD'S RICHES

Published by Spire Resources Inc.
PO Box 180, Camarillo, CA 93011
1-800-992-3060

Cover and text design by Bill Thielker

Printed in the United States of America

ISBN 0-9715828-4-X

INTRODUCTION

The number 33 appears several times in the Bible...

Jacob had 33 children.

King David reigned over Israel for 33 years.

Jesus was 33 years old when He gave His life for us.

It's a fascinating number, and now we're going to experience it in a very special way. For 33 eventful days, in a collective effort involving the entire church family, we'll discover the full meaning of stewardship. It will be a journey we'll long remember.

This important emphasis, called *33 Days of Stewardship,* is intended to guide us into a deeper understanding of what it means to be disciples of Jesus Christ. We'll explore all the dimensions of stewardship — the management of everything that God entrusts to us.

An Essential Emphasis

To understand stewardship is to grasp the essence of life's meaning. To practice stewardship is to fulfill that meaning in a way that pleases God and satisfies the most profound human longings.

Over these 33 days we'll have both a corporate and a personal strategy. When we come together, there will be sermons and lessons on the theme of total-life stewardship. On our own, we'll take a few minutes each day to read, reflect and respond to one aspect of stewardship. It's a simple plan, but it's going to make a major impact.

A Daily Plan with Daily Power

The Daily Plan for the *33 Days of Stewardship* includes two basic resources:

The 33 Laws of Stewardship

The *33 Days of Stewardship* Discovery Guide

The 33 Laws of Stewardship is an acclaimed book which examines 33 principles of stewardship. These are Laws established in God's character and expressed in His Word. The chapters are brief, but they're inspiring and insightful.

This booklet, the *33 Days of Stewardship* Discovery Guide, is a companion to the book. It's designed with a basic "3 R's" format — a daily Reading, a daily Reflection, and a daily Response. The daily Reading is one chapter in the book. The daily Reflection is one vital thought to consider. And the daily Response may be a question to answer, an action to take, an example to follow or a prayer to make your own. For most people, the "3 R's" will take no more than 10-15 minutes each day to complete.

As we follow this Daily Plan we'll grow in wisdom and gain in understanding. The ultimate purpose of the *33 Days of Stewardship* is for us to be highly effective, faith-driven stewards of Jesus Christ. This is possible because of His promise: We can do all things through Him who strengthens us!

Get ready for the blessing and benefit of these life-changing 33 Days!

DAY
1

TODAY'S READING

Chapter 1: The Law of Rightful Ownership

Key Thought: *Nothing truly belongs to us; everything actually belongs to God.*

TODAY'S REFLECTION

When we are blessed with money and material things, and when we receive acclaim for any accomplishment, we're getting not what we deserve, but what God in His grace lovingly allows us to enjoy and to care for. The essence of life is not ownership but stewardship — the faithful management of all that God entrusts to us. Some of us are entrusted with a lot, some with a little; but whatever comes to us brings with it an undeniable responsibility. The temptation is to think that abundance is found in possessing life's benefits, when actually it's discovered in stewarding life's blessings.

TODAY'S RESPONSE

As a part of their financial planning, many people place their assets in a trust, a vehicle that holds and administers those assets to maximize the benefits for all concerned. God has given you some of His assets to hold in trust for Him, to manage for His glory and benefit as well as for your own blessing and well-being. Take a few moments to think about the assets God has entrusted to you. On the lines below, describe some of those things; then, as an expression of faith, affirm your trust agreement with God by signing your name at the bottom of the page.

I, _____ ,
recognize that God is the rightful owner of all the assets I call my own, such as my:

_____

_____

I also recognize that God has entrusted these things to me to use for His honor and glory. I believe that He will provide everything I need as I faithfully use what He has given for His purposes, and so I freely and gladly acknowledge that I am His steward, His trustee.

(Signed) _____

DAY
2

TODAY'S READING

Chapter 2: The Law of Purposeful Possession

Key Thought: *Wise stewards are guided by Lordship, not "hoardship."*

TODAY'S REFLECTION

No one sets out to be like the rich fool in the parable in Luke 12. But the pull to hang on to things for one's personal benefit is strong, especially in an uncertain, materialistic world. Jesus gives the only alternative: become rich toward God. How? By concentrating on giving to God rather than getting for self. This kind of generosity is the only known antidote to greed and it presents a powerful demonstration of our belief in His Lordship. If we really believe He is Lord of all and that He will care for us as He promised, our grip on the things of this life will be loosened and we can begin to operate as stewards rather than as hoarders.

TODAY'S RESPONSE

What do you think we're trying to accomplish by our rush to acquire, accumulate and hoard wealth and possessions?

How would bringing God into the equation change those motivations?

What is one step you can take today to move from "hoardship" to "Lordship" in the way you view your money, possessions, opportunities and talents?

DAY 3

TODAY'S READING

Chapter 3: The Law of Miraculous Multiplication

Key Thought: *The economics of stewardship is governed by the mathematics of the supernatural.*

TODAY'S REFLECTION

What do you think? Would the food have arrived at the door of the Müller orphanage had he not prayed, believing God for His provision?

Skeptics will say we can never really know. But we do know that 120 hungry orphans had full stomachs that night. And we do know that thousands of people have read the story of George Müller's faith and been encouraged to trust God in their own circumstances, seeing Him supply their needs in often miraculous ways as well. Who could ever have imagined that one man's commitment to live by faith would have such multiplied results?

It's true that we are called to walk by faith, not by sight — that there are things we will not see, things we will not understand, things we will simply have to accept and act on as true. But it's also true that when we choose to exercise faith in the stewardship of life, God responds according to the mathematics of the supernatural, giving far beyond what is imagined, providing far beyond what is expected and blessing far beyond what is deserved. It's math of the most miraculous kind!

TODAY'S RESPONSE

Think of a major need you are facing right now. How can you, like George Müller, demonstrate faith and confidence in God's promise regarding your need?

DAY 4

TODAY'S READING

Chapter 4: The Law of Guaranteed Return

Key Thought: *As you give so it will be given to you.*

TODAY'S REFLECTION

The Laws of Stewardship are rooted in the immovable ground of God's promises. They are sure and certain, truths that we can count on. They are the absolutely positive teaching of Jesus, such as the Law of Guaranteed Return that He stated like this: "Give, and it will be given to you," He said, "a good measure, pressed down, shaken together and running over, will be poured into your lap. For with the measure you use, it will be measured to you." (Luke 6:38)

The purpose behind this promise is that we be motivated to give because it's a sensible investment. Spiritually speaking, there's virtually no risk but all reward. Any gift given for God's glory is backed by the infinite resources of the Bank of Heaven. There is no doubt about it, no cause for concern, no conditions under which the return is held back or held up. It will come.

TODAY'S RESPONSE

How would you describe the "measure" you've been using in your giving? Is it an eyedropper...a teaspoon...a cup...a bucket...a barrel?

Take a moment to honestly search your heart in the light of Luke 6:38. Prayerfully ask the Lord to reveal anything that might be holding you back from giving more fully and freely to Him. Ask Him to increase the "measure" of your faith and your giving.

DAY
5

TODAY'S READING

Chapter 5: The Law of Hilarious Generosity

Key Thought: *God loves givers who give with the right attitude.*

TODAY'S REFLECTION

Take a moment to do what today's chapter suggests:
Imagine the feelings of the disciples when Jesus took those five loaves of bread and two fish and turned them into a feast for thousands. Think of the hilarious joy they felt handing out food to the hungry, seeing God multiply it as long as they kept sharing. What a beautiful picture of what it's like for us when we give from the endless resources He entrusts to us.

TODAY'S RESPONSE

Describe a time when you were prompted to give, but either talked yourself out of giving or allowed the opportunity to pass without following through on the prompting in your heart. What was the effect of that experience?

_____

_____

_____

_____

_____

Describe a time when you were a channel of blessing like the disciples, when you passed on something God had given you. What was that experience like for you?

_____

_____

_____

_____

DAY 6

TODAY'S READING

Chapter 6: The Law of Faithful Dependability

Key Thought: *Trustworthiness marks the true steward.*

TODAY'S REFLECTION

Faithful dependability as a Christian steward relates to the management of money, but also to a great deal more. The "portfolio" for which we are responsible includes a wide range of components, and God's expectation is that we make the most of each one. Think of all the "assets" you have under management: your money, your time, your possessions, your opportunities, your influence, your relationships and much more. And to this long list can be added the spiritual assets with which we are entrusted: the gospel of Christ, the mystery of godliness, the secret things of God. This is no small responsibility we bear, and to handle it rightly demands absolute faithfulness.

TODAY'S RESPONSE

In Today's Reflection a number of "assets" are listed: Money. Time. Possessions. Opportunities. Influence. Relationships. The Gospel. The Word of God. Each of these assets has the potential for multiplied spiritual value. It all depends upon how they are managed. Through wise, faithful stewardship each one can grow in worth and increase in impact. For example, money can be given to fund God-honoring projects. Opportunities can be seized to meet vital needs. The Gospel can be shared to guide people to the Savior. This is the compelling reality of biblical stewardship: how we manage makes a difference, often an eternal difference. Select an "asset" from the eight listed above and describe how you're going to manage that asset today for God's glory.

DAY
7

TODAY'S READING

Chapter 7: The Law of Paradoxical Participation

Key Thought: *The richest generosity often comes out of the deepest poverty.*

TODAY'S REFLECTION

What tremendous examples of generosity are described in today's chapter! The Macedonians, in severe straits themselves, poverty-stricken and persecuted, yet out of the joy in their hearts, giving to help the brothers and sisters in Jerusalem they had never even seen. And John Wesley, so intent upon giving away everything he was given as he served the Lord that he died with only £10 to his name. They both remind us that as believers we truly are called to be rivers, not reservoirs. We are channels, not containers, of the gracious supply God pours out upon us, no matter what our particular situation may be. Remaining open to the needs of others even when you are in need yourself is a constant challenge for the child of God. But that kind of open heart and open hand places you in very good company with an itinerant preacher and some first century believers who have gone before you and set an important example.

TODAY'S RESPONSE

Do you have something in common with the Macedonian believers? Is there a place in your life where you are being humbled, persecuted or placed in great need? Describe it briefly.

_____

_____

_____

_____

_____

Ask God to show you someone who has the same kind of need you face. Prayerfully consider how you might help them — not for what it will bring you in return, but so that you can be a channel, not a container, of God's gracious supply.

DAY 8

TODAY'S READING

Chapter 8: The Law of Supernatural Supply

Key Thought: *God enables the giver to give beyond the ability to give.*

TODAY'S REFLECTION

The core power of the Christian life is supernatural. When it comes to giving, many Christians forget this or simply fail to understand the spiritual reality. While we have to be detail-conscious in our record-keeping and bottom-line-conscious in our spending, God's ability to supply is not limited by the structures of our accounting systems or the projections of our financial planning software. Unfortunately, those who give to the Lord's work sometimes become more aware of what is lacking rather than what is available through the abundance of God's supply. God calls us to give far beyond what we think we can because He promises to be the source of what we have to give. His supernatural supply must underwrite all our thoughts and attitudes about stewardship.

TODAY'S RESPONSE

What has been your "comfort zone" when it comes to giving?

_____

_____

_____

_____

Are you willing to ask God to move you out of your "comfort zone" and enable you to give exceedingly, abundantly above what you've experienced before? Check the box that best describes where you are today:

❏ I'm ready for God to move me out of my "comfort zone"

❏ I'm still praying for more faith to make this move

❏ I'm not yet ready to be moved

DAY
9

TODAY'S READING

Chapter 9: The Law of Eager Willingness

Key Thought: *Wise stewards joyfully choose to support God's work and do God's will.*

TODAY'S REFLECTION

In stewardship, choice is a never-ending concern, for we must constantly decide how to manage everything that God puts in our care. Most important of all is that we decide with true purpose, joyfully choosing to support God's work and do God's will. Paul commended the Christians at Corinth for having this attitude: "You were the first not only to give but also to have the desire to do so. Now finish the work, so that your eager willingness to do it may be matched by your completion of it, according to your means. For if the willingness is there, the gift is acceptable according to what one has, not according to what he does not have." (2 Corinthians 8:10-12).

TODAY'S RESPONSE

How would you describe your usual response when you are asked to give toward the Lord's work?

What do you think is the secret to having an "eager willingness" to give?

What is one step you could take in developing and maintaining a more "eager willingness" in giving?

DAY
10

TODAY'S READING

Chapter 10: The Law of Reciprocal Supply

Key Thought: *Through meeting others' needs we meet our own.*

TODAY'S REFLECTION

Christian stewardship is not fulfilled in a vacuum. It is not merely an individual responsibility, for we belong to one another and must think of one another, not just ourselves. To live by the Law of Reciprocal Supply is to maintain an upward and outward attitude, not an inward focus.

TODAY'S RESPONSE

Today's chapter reminds us of the absolute importance of spiritual gifts in the exercise of stewardship. What are the primary spiritual gifts you believe God has given you?

Give an example of how you are currently using your gifts to minister within the church body.

Is there someone with a need that you're aware of? Has God placed you in a position to meet their need? Write their name and describe their need below, then pray for wisdom to meet it most effectively.

DAY 11

TODAY'S READING

Chapter 11: The Law of Constructive Contribution

Key Thought: *The work of God is to be done by the people of God giving according to the will of God.*

TODAY'S REFLECTION

John Wesley's reminder to his parishioner perfectly sums up the Law of Constructive Contribution: "Go and read the third chapter of Nehemiah and learn that he who repaired the dung gate was counted of as much honor as he who worked on the gate of the fountain. All did their bit; you and I can do no more."

As a believer and as a member of this church body, you are standing shoulder to shoulder with others in the work of God. You are not working alone. But you are making a contribution that no one else can make. You have a place to fill, a role to play that no one else can. Without a doubt, you will encounter opposition. Your personal circumstances may seem to conspire against your successful completion of the task before you. You may be criticized by others who don't like how you're doing your part. You may even begin to question the worth of what you're doing. Do what Nehemiah did. Pray. Set your defenses against the opposition. And keep going. Fulfill your role with confidence in God and persistence in doing good. Don't let your part of the wall remain undone. You will be rewarded.

TODAY'S RESPONSE

What do you see as your role in the ongoing work of God through our church? What part of the "wall" will you endeavor to build?

DAY 12

TODAY'S READING

Chapter 12: The Law of Purposeful Blessing

Key Thought: *We are made rich in every way to be generous on every occasion.*

TODAY'S REFLECTION

Those six words William Borden penned during his short life speak volumes to us about the true nature of stewardship: No Reserves. No Retreats. No Regrets. Blessed both materially and spiritually, William found his greatest joy in passing along those blessings to others at every opportunity. Even as he set his heart on reaching the multitudes in other parts of the world, he reached out to bless everyone around him, from the homeless drunks on the streets of New Haven to the privileged students in the dormitories and classrooms of Yale University. He had found his purpose in life: to honor God with everything he possessed. The place and the particular recipients of his blessing were secondary. His obedience was the joyful response of a grateful heart overflowing to everyone around him. How perfectly he understood that we are blessed with a purpose: to in turn bless others on purpose — deliberately, thoughtfully and joyfully.

TODAY'S RESPONSE

What is one specific way God has "made you rich" this past year?

_____

_____

_____

_____

How have you been (or how will you be) generous with that particular blessing?

_____

_____

_____

_____

DAY 13

TODAY'S READING

Chapter 13: The Law of Consistent Collection

Key Thought: *Consistent giving facilitates consistent ministry.*

TODAY'S REFLECTION

Paul's instruction in 1 Corinthians 16:1-3 isn't a legalistic demand that we give a certain amount of money every week to the Lord's work. It is simply a recognition that the needs of the body can be met in a decent and orderly fashion, without a lot of fuss or fanfare. The offering he was referring to was a one-time collection for the suffering saints in Jerusalem. But many needs in the church are not so dramatic. Electric bills must be paid. Buildings and equipment must be maintained for good steward-ship. The salaries of faithful workers must be met. Those kinds of ongoing needs require ongoing support. That's where consistent, regular giving is so important. And what we put in the offering each week is just as much an act of worship and expression of devotion as the songs we sing or the Scriptures we study in a church service. Giving regularly is a wonderful demonstration of His Lordship over our resources and our gratitude to Him for His consistent, unfailing care of us.

TODAY'S RESPONSE

Think back over the last year. Was your giving to the Lord's work more or less than you planned to give? What might explain the difference?

_____

_____

_____

Think about the next year. Is God directing you to give in a differ-ent way or with a different purpose? What is He impressing upon your heart?

_____

_____

_____

DAY 14

TODAY'S READING

Chapter 14: The Law of Proportionate Participation

Key Thought: *God's provision dictates the believer's proportion.*

TODAY'S REFLECTION

This law teaches us that God's provision dictates the believer's proportion. In other words, what He provides determines what we give. If he gives a little, from that little we are to give; if He gives abundantly, from that abundance we are to give. Whatever He provides, regardless of the depth or breadth, determines the measure of our giving.

Proportionate participation in the work of God involves much more than money. Whatever God has given you, in whatever measure, is to be dedicated to Him. Your talents, your abilities, your material wealth, your time — all are resources from which you can give.

TODAY'S RESPONSE

What do your own records reveal about the proportion of your giving? Approximately what percentage of your income was given to the Lord last year?

_____ %

Over the next 12 months, are you resolved to change this percentage in some way? If so, what portion of your income are you determining to give to advance the Lord's work through His church?

_____ %

Whatever number you've written above, take a few moments to thank God for His provision, to acknowledge His empowerment, and to ask for His enablement to increase your giving for His sake.

DAY
15

TODAY'S READING

Chapter 15: The Law of Personal Initiative

Key Thought: *Desire precedes duty in the grace of giving.*

TODAY'S REFLECTION

In Christ, we have been liberated eternally. And because of the freedom He has given us, we are able to give wholeheartedly and unreservedly to Him. He allows us to exercise this freedom by our own determination. That was the principle at work in the Macedonians when they gave "entirely on their own." They took the initiative in giving, exercising their freedom in an expression of true generosity.

Jesus doesn't force us to be His disciples. Never does He coerce anyone into His service. His invitation is free, His offer of eternal life is free, the indwelling of His Spirit is free, the opportunity to serve Him is free. He has given beyond all measure, all at His personal initiative. How can we not as stewards live by the Law of Personal Initiative and choose willingly to give our all for Him?

TODAY'S RESPONSE

Giving out of a sense of duty is good. Coupling that sense of duty with a passionate desire to give is better. And adding to these a deep, appreciative love for the Lord is the absolute best. Take a few moments to talk to the Lord about why you give to His work. As you pray, ask Him to increase your willingness to obey Him, to increase your desire to please Him, and to increase your love in giving for Him.

DAY
16

TODAY'S READING

Chapter 16: The Law of Total Excellence

Key Thought: *Excellence in giving is part of a matched set of virtues.*

TODAY'S REFLECTION

In the Apostle Paul's second letter to the believers in Corinth, he describes a complete set of ideals, and he urges them to have the whole collection as it were: "But just as you excel in everything — in faith, in speech, in knowledge, in complete earnestness and in your love for us — see that you also excel in this grace of giving." (2 Corinthians 8:7) This verse describes a matched set of virtues, a combination of qualities that epitomize all that is best: excellence in what one believes, says, knows, desires, feels and gives. For the believer, living a life of excellence is paramount, for it reflects the pure perfection of God.

Excellence should characterize the servant of Jesus Christ, and it should be thoroughly evident in our stewardship. The Law of Total Excellence reinforces this priority, teaching us to always pursue the highest and best, never settling for mediocrity. Take a look at the men and women of faith in Scripture and it's crystal clear that they were people who excelled.

TODAY'S RESPONSE

Think about the three essential points in the conclusion to Chapter 16: 1. Discipline yourself to give. 2. Determine to give daily. 3. Devote yourself to the Giver. All three are vital to a life of spiritual excellence; but the highest priority is the final point: Devotion to the Giver. Giving is, above all, an act of worship. Remember this the next time (and, hopefully, every time) you write a check to the church or place money in the offering. Tell yourself, This is a gift to the One who has given all to me.

If you haven't already done so, memorize the words of Jesus in Matthew 6:19-21: "Do not store up for yourselves treasures on earth, where moth and rust destroy, and where thieves break in and steal. But store up for yourselves treasures in heaven, where moth and rust do not destroy, and where thieves do not break in and steal. For where your treasure is, there your heart will be also."

DAY 17

TODAY'S READING

Chapter 17: The Law of Rightful Reward

Key Thought: *Reward for stewardship and service is granted by God, not gained by man.*

TODAY'S REFLECTION

Remembering the Law of Rightful Reward helps us maintain the right heart attitude as we give and serve. We can very easily slip into the mindset of Peter or the first group of laborers, calculating "what's in it for me" or, unconsciously and subtly, beginning to demand or dictate to God how He keeps His promises to us.

How much better to serve with complete and utter trust in the master's proposition: "Go, and whatever is right I will give you. Is it not lawful for me to do what I wish with my own things?" God's promises of provision and reward are sure and He will give us far more than we deserve; but only if our motives are pure and our hearts are fixed on Him, not on the reward He brings.

TODAY'S RESPONSE

Some of the laborers in Jesus' parable made the mistake of wrongly comparing themselves with other workers. Have you ever fallen into the trap of getting your eyes off the Lord and comparing yourself with other Christians? If so, what was the result?

What means the most to you in the statement, "Go, and whatever is right I will give you"? How does this influence your living and giving?

DAY 18

TODAY'S READING

Chapter 18: The Law of Zealous Readiness

Key Thought: *Zealous stewardship spreads like a powerful contagion.*

TODAY'S REFLECTION

Simon the Zealot must have been an exciting person to be around. That kind of passionate, enthusiastic personality can't remain still or quiet for very long. And it probably didn't take a great deal of time for those around him to observe and hear about what was important to him — and be caught up in it, too. He couldn't keep it contained. It just spilled out of him.

We can't really hide our genuine passions, either. They reveal themselves in what we talk about, how we spend our time, how we spend our resources. And we can't really keep them from affecting those around us. Just as the Corinthians' eager readiness to give inspired the Macedonians to give in spite of their poverty, our zealous stewardship can ignite an entire body of believers to give "far beyond their abilities" and devote themselves wholly to the Lord. That's just how it works.

TODAY'S RESPONSE

What would an honest evaluation of how you spend your time, your energies and your resources lead someone to conclude about what is important to you?

Are you becoming more passionate about knowing God, serving Him and giving to His work? What is increasing that passion, and how can you keep it kindled?

DAY
19

TODAY'S READING

Chapter 19: The Law of Graceful Abundance

Key Thought: *Abundant grace brings abundant blessing and spurs abundant ministry.*

TODAY'S REFLECTION

God's promise is limitless: He is able to make *all* grace abound toward us. His grace is relevant in *all* things at *all* times. He will provide *all* that we need. He will enable us to abound in *every* good work. There is no reason under any circumstances for us as believers to ever feel spiritually limited. Those two words alone — *all* and *every* — should be sufficient reminders of His power at work in us and for us.

TODAY'S RESPONSE

Think of a recent time when God's grace was very evident in your life. Imagine that the lines below are a "memorial stone" like those that Joshua put up for the people of Israel as a reminder of God's power and provision. Describe your experience and then ask God for an opportunity to share that story of His grace with someone who really needs it.

DAY 20

TODAY'S READING

Chapter 20: The Law of Secret Spirituality

Key Thought: *Godly giving is a private demonstration, not a public display.*

TODAY'S REFLECTION

With rare exceptions, giving is to be a private demonstration of obedience, not a public display of magnanimity. God is pleased when a gift is given with regard only for the Lord, completely devoid of any attention being drawn to the giver. To draw attention to oneself when giving is to express an attitude of ownership rather than stewardship. If you think that what you are giving is something you own instead of something that has been entrusted to you, you have eliminated God from the equation. The wise steward never forgets that everything belongs to God and every gift is facilitated by Him alone.

TODAY'S RESPONSE

Have you ever seen anyone draw attention to themselves with a public display of their generosity? If so, how did it make you feel and what did it make you think?

_____

_____

_____

_____

Knowing yourself, what is one thing you might do to remind yourself that giving is for God to be glorified, not for others to be impressed?

_____

_____

_____

_____

DAY 21

TODAY'S READING

Chapter 21: The Law of Sacrificial Example

Key Thought: *The most significant gifts are often given by the most insignificant givers.*

TODAY'S REFLECTION

A despised Samaritan. One of the most insignificant people in the scheme of life 2,000 years ago. But his example of sacrificial giving continues to inspire believers two millennia later.

The Samaritan's philosophy – *What's Mine is Yours* – permeated his actions and his attitudes. His behavior set an example we are to follow today as we live out the Law of Sacrificial Example in our stewardship. Our challenge is to look at our lives and ask honestly, what would God have me give sacrificially for His sake? There are people in desperate need today — physically, emotionally and spiritually desperate — and God uses people to meet such needs. As the Samaritan's actions saved a man's life, we too can be instruments used of God in His miraculous work of redemption. As true believers it is imperative that we look at all of our resources and say resoundingly, Lord, *What's Mine is Yours!* This must be our philosophy, for without this spirit of sacrifice we cannot and will not mature and succeed spiritually.

TODAY'S RESPONSE

"Lord, What's Mine is Yours!" How will you live by this philosophy and demonstrate this attitude? Describe a specific way you'll show this in supporting the church, helping a needy person or interceding for a fellow Christian.

DAY 22

TODAY'S READING

Chapter 22: The Law of Over-the-Top Offerings

Key Thought: *Blessed believers live and give above and beyond.*

TODAY'S REFLECTION

In many churches, as with many Christians, major financial needs cause major emotional stress. It shouldn't be this way. God doesn't intend it and we shouldn't do it. The best way to keep from going "over the edge" in facing a need is to go "over-the-top" in making an offering — both in quantity and quality. Moses had to restrain the people from giving because there was more than enough to complete the task. That's quantity! David had spent much of his reign gathering the very finest gold, silver, bronze, wood, stone and marble for the Temple. Then, when the work was ready to commence, he opened up his own personal treasuries — the best of the best — and added his bounty to the resources. That's quality! The Tabernacle was completed and the Temple was built because people who knew they had been blessed by God gave far beyond what was necessary for the work. They didn't see the need as a problem or a pain, but as an opportunity to glorify God and build His kingdom; and they were hugely blessed in the process.

TODAY'S RESPONSE

What kind of "over-the-top" offering is God calling on you to make?

DAY
23

TODAY'S READING

Chapter 23: The Law of Unified Commitment

Key Thought: *Oneness of heart and mind brings greatness of power and witness.*

TODAY'S REFLECTION

Look again at that description of the Christians in Acts 4: "All the believers were one in heart and mind. No one claimed that any of his possessions was his own, but they shared everything they had. With great power the apostles continued to testify to the resurrection of the Lord Jesus, and much grace was upon them all."(Acts 4:32-33)

God's design and His desire is that we work in spiritual partnership, not as sole proprietors. "Lone rangers" cannot experience the exhilaration of spiritual unity. And when a congregation is truly united in service and stewardship, the impact is powerful. Unity of this kind turns a body of believers into a spiritual force for righteousness.

TODAY'S RESPONSE

• Fellow Christians as partners, not competitors.
• Gifts to the Lord's work as contributions to a unique mutual fund.
• The church as a powerful laser beam, not a collection of light bulbs.

What role can you play to encourage this kind of unity in the church body?

DAY 24

TODAY'S READING

Chapter 24: The Law of Risky Mismanagement

Key Thought: *Trying to trick God will always trip you up.*

TODAY'S REFLECTION

In His dealings with Ananias and Sapphira, God was teaching the church that He wants a Spirit-led surrender. Nothing fake, nothing contrived; for we have to be honest with Him and with one another. When we mismanage what He has entrusted to us, taking selfish risks with His resources, the consequences can be frightening. It isn't that God is waiting for an opportunity to punish us; but He is watching and He is judging, and we will be held accountable for our stewardship. When we violate His principles, especially when we make ourselves out to be better Christians than we really are, a kind of death occurs — the death that separates us from fellowship with God and with one another.

TODAY'S RESPONSE

What are some ways we pretend to be better Christians than we really are?

_____

_____

_____

_____

What helps you to be real before God and others?

_____

_____

_____

_____

DAY 25

TODAY'S READING

Chapter 25: The Law of Heartful Humility

Key Thought: *Putting others first makes an impact that will last.*

TODAY'S REFLECTION

Excellent stewards consistently choose to put others first. Even though they may be remarkable individuals with exceptional skills, they choose not to blow their own horns. Willingly and lovingly, they humble themselves. Jonathan was willing both to give and to give up in order that God's will be done. He lovingly yielded his resources. He boldly intervened and interceded for David, knowing that the young man was God's chosen servant. He set aside his "rights" and sought the higher good. In all these ways, Jonathan is an example to us as believers today.

TODAY'S RESPONSE

Would you truly be willing, like Jonathan, to support someone else's success if it meant you would have to take a lower position? Answer and comment.

How might you ensure that your concern is more for the church's health and success than for your own role in helping that to happen?

DAY 26

TODAY'S READING

Chapter 26: The Law of Unconditional Contentment

Key Thought: *The steward's contentment is not dependent upon the steward's circumstances.*

TODAY'S REFLECTION

There is one thing you can almost always count on about circumstances: they are bound to change. Paul's certainly did. He said, "I know what it is to be in need and I know what it is to have plenty." And he apparently had figured out how to weather the change from one to the other without a lot of fuss. He went on to say, "I have learned the secret of being content in any and every situation, whether well fed or hungry, whether living in plenty or in want." What's the secret? Knowing that Christ is there in that situation with us. That enables us to be content…because when we have Him, we have everything we need.

TODAY'S RESPONSE

Think about a situation or circumstance you are struggling with right now. Take a moment to pray this prayer:

Lord, thank You for being with me in [describe the situation]

I confess that I don't have the wisdom or the strength in myself to handle this, but I also confess my absolute confidence that You will give me everything I need to live for You in it. I choose to find my contentment in You, in Your presence and Your strength in my life, not in my circumstances. Amen.

DAY 27

TODAY'S READING

Chapter 27: The Law of Pastoral Provision

Key Thought: *God's people must take care of God's servants.*

TODAY'S REFLECTION

Philippians 4:19 is frequently quoted in sermons and lessons about stewardship. It's a tremendous promise: God will supply all our needs according to His riches in Christ Jesus. But have you ever noticed the context? This wonderful assurance of God's provision was given to a group of believers who themselves had been providing for someone else — the servant of God who brought them the Gospel, the apostle Paul.

Scripture makes it very clear: those who are ministered to need to take care of those who minister to them. Physically, emotionally, spiritually — in every way, we are to care for, encourage and enable those God has placed in spiritual leadership in the church. Theirs is a heavy burden of responsibility. They have much to watch out for and care for. And one day, they will stand before the Lord to answer for how they ministered to us. How can we not encourage them and help them carry out the ministry God has given them?

TODAY'S RESPONSE

What is one thing you can do to help care for and show your appreciation for the church's spiritual leaders? Describe it, then determine to do it.

DAY 28

TODAY'S READING

Chapter 28: The Law of Godly Contentment

Key Thought: *Wise stewards are happy with what they have, not hassled by what they don't have.*

TODAY'S REFLECTION

Read again Paul's words to Timothy: "Godliness with contentment is great gain, for we brought nothing into the world and we can take nothing out of it. But if we have food and clothing, we will be content with that." (1 Timothy 6:6-8) This entire section of Paul's letter to Timothy is brimming with the idea, "Live simply. Hold onto things lightly. Don't get caught up in the pursuit of money or the accumulation of possessions. It's a trap. It will only bring you grief." Gratitude for the essentials in life...freedom from materialistic hungers...contentment in the provision of God...these are the marks of a wise (and happy) steward.

TODAY'S RESPONSE

Have you ever gotten caught up in the pursuit of "more" when you actually already had "enough"? Describe how it happened and how you felt.

_____

_____

_____

_____

What are some ways we can assure ourselves of "having enough" and being content?

_____

_____

_____

_____

DAY 29

TODAY'S READING

Chapter 29: The Law of Future-Focused Giving

Key Thought: *Wise stewards invest for the longest possible term.*

TODAY'S REFLECTION

Among the "I" problems of the rich fool in Luke 12 was this one: he was terribly shortsighted. Blessed beyond his expectations, the only thing he could think to do with his bounty was to make his earthly life more comfortable and secure. Somehow he never looked beyond the present to see how his wealth could affect eternity! He totally missed the opportunity to invest for the long-term that Paul later described to Timothy as, "...lay[ing] up treasure for themselves as a firm foundation for the coming age, so that they may take hold of the life that is truly life" (1 Timothy 6:19). Missing that, he missed everything.

TODAY'S RESPONSE

Are you being far-sighted in your use of what God has given you? Describe how you're using or purposing to use your resources for more than this present life's needs.

_____

_____

_____

_____

_____

_____

_____

_____

_____

_____

_____

_____

DAY 30

TODAY'S READING

Chapter 30: The Law of Absolute Harvest

Key Thought: *Sow sparingly, reap sparingly; sow bountifully, reap bountifully.*

TODAY'S REFLECTION

God gives us a supply of "seed" to be planted for His purposes. Whatever He supplies to you, sow it generously and wisely. The spiritual harvest will come. It is a well-defined, well-ordered process that is in God's hands, not our own. We till the ground, we sow the seed, we cultivate the plants, but God gives the increase, for He and He alone is Lord of the Harvest.

TODAY'S RESPONSE

What kind of harvest do you think you can expect from the "seed" you've sown in the past year?

What are you determining to sow in the year to come?

DAY 31

TODAY'S READING

Chapter 31: The Law of Single-minded Service

Key Thought: *One can serve God or serve money; no one can serve both.*

TODAY'S REFLECTION

Being single-minded means "having a single focus, a single interest, a single purpose. It implies exclusivity of devotion, a wholehearted commitment to God transcending all other commitments." Not easy to do in this frantic, materialistic world we live in. It's so very easy to become distracted and fragmented in our hearts as well as in our actions. Remaining focused on serving God requires self-denial, sacrifice and perseverance. It isn't easy, but it is the only way for a faithful steward to live.

TODAY'S RESPONSE

What are the biggest distractions to single-minded service you are facing right now?

How can you bring life back into proper focus?

DAY 32

TODAY'S READING

Chapter 32: The Law of Channeled Resources

Key Thought: *Stewards are the channels of an endless, eternal supply.*

TODAY'S REFLECTION

As a steward, you have the incredible privilege of being a conduit of God's love, grace and power. He wants to use you as a vehicle through which to bring glory to Himself. Whatever He gives you in terms of resources is to be channeled, not dammed up and stored for personal benefit. The more open you are, the more blessed you will be and the more His grace will flow out to the world around you. And no matter how much you pass on, there will always be more available.

TODAY'S RESPONSE

How "open" would you say you've been as a channel of God's love, grace and power? What can you do today to increase that openness?

DAY 33

TODAY'S READING

Chapter 33: The Law of Loving Compliance

Key Thought: *Pure obedience prompted by pure love produces pure stewardship.*

TODAY'S REFLECTION

Just as Jesus' purpose was to do the Father's will, so is ours. His saving work is done. But our serving work continues because we are called to do the Father's will until our days are ended. No coercion, no guilt motivation, just pure love spilling out as wholehearted obedience that results in effective stewardship of all His blessings. That's how we run the race, fixing our eyes on the One waiting at the finish line and longing to hear Him say, "Well done, good and faithful servant.

TODAY'S RESPONSE

What do you need to lay aside or throw off in order to run the race God has destined for you?

_____

_____

_____

_____

_____

_____

_____

_____

_____

As you run for His glory, remember this prayer:

Lord, help me to run in your power and not my own, to fix my eyes on you alone, to give my all as a servant and steward. Empower me to race toward the line with a pure, compliant heart that beats with passion for your Kingdom. In Jesus' Name, Amen.